World's Silliest Jokes

Philip Yates
& Matt Rissinger

Illustrated by Jeff Sinclair

ublishing Co., Inc.
New York

To Uncle Francis and Aunt Maria. Lots of love and laughs. –P.Y.

To Dad. Your sense of humor has improved.–M.R.

Library of Congress Cataloging-in-Publication Data
Rissinger, Matt.
    World's silliest jokes / Matt Rissinger & Philip Yates ;
illustrated by Jeff Sinclair
      p.   cm.
  Includes index
  Summary: Hundreds of jokes, puns, riddles, and other witticisms.
  ISBN 0-8069-4884-1
    1. Riddles, Juvenile. 2. Wit and humor, Juvenile. [1. Riddles. 2.
Jokes. 3. Puns and punning. 4. Wit and humor.] I. Yates, Philip,
1956- . II. Sinclair, Jeff, ill. III. Title.
PN6731.5.R57 1997
818'.5402–dc20   96-35452
                              CIP
                              AC

10 9 8 7 6 5 4 3

First paperback edition published in 1998 by
Sterling Publishing Company, Inc.
387 Park Avenue South, New York, N.Y. 10016
© 1997 by Philip Yates and Matt Rissinger
Illustrations © 1997 by Jeff Sinclair
Distributed in Canada by Sterling Publishing
% Canadian Manda Group, One Atlantic Avenue, Suite 105
Toronto, Ontario, Canada M6K 3E7
Distributed in Australia by Capricorn Link (Australia) Pty Ltd.
P.O. Box 6651, Baulkham Hills, Business Centre, NSW 2153, Australia
Manufactured in the United States of America
All rights reserved

Sterling ISBN 0-8069-4884-1 Trade
              0-8069-4885-X Paper

Contents

1. ANIMAL CRACK-UPS

MOE: How is a Doberman in the desert like a frank-furter?

JOE: I don't know.

MOE: They're both hot dogs.

My dog is so lazy, he hires other dogs to chase cats for him.

FRAN: My dog can chase a stick for three miles.

DAN: Sounds far-fetched.

LLOYD: What's gray and red and never stops laughing?

FLOYD: An elephant tickled pink.

BENNY: What comes with a tiny cage and eats stir-fry?
LENNY: A Pet Wok.

SLIM: When birds pick football teams, why are the
    ducks always chosen before anybody else?
TIM: Because they're good at making first downs.

FUNNY FE-LINES

FLIP: What goes "Meow-meow, quack-quack,
    munch-munch"?
FLOP: A duck-filled fatty puss.

FLIP: What do you call a cat that eats an elephant?
FLOP: Full.

Why did the sea bird rob the jewelry store?
Because diamonds are a gull's best friend.

What's big and gray and bumps into buildings?
A near-sighted elephant.

What's big and gray with a white stripe on its trunk?
An elephant wearing sunblock.

What's gray, weighs two tons, and puts you to sleep?
A hypno-potamus.

RUDY: Where do dogs wash their clothes?
JUDY: At the laundro-mutt.

How do otters get around when the river dries up?
They drive otter-mobiles.

TERRY: How do you keep the cat from sleeping in your bed?
KERRY: I do what I have to when puss comes to shove.

What do you get if you cross a dog with a chicken?
Pooched eggs.

PATIENT: Doc, I think I'm a giraffe.
DOCTOR: Isn't that stretching it a bit?

CHAD: What do you call a large ocean mammal with a bad dye job?
BRAD: A bleached whale.

CHICKIE: What do you get if you cross an elephant and a rooster?
DICKIE: An animal that never forgets to wake you up in the morning.

FLO: Why do you never see zebras in the army?
JOE: Because they've already earned their stripes.

What would you get if you crossed a blimp with an orangutan?
A hot air baboon.

Did you hear about the duck who had so many older brothers that he always got the hand-me-downs?

MOE: Why did the chicken cross the road at Disneyland?
JOE: To get to the other ride.

Mother Horse to Father Horse: "I don't care if it was your father's name, we are not calling our new son Charlie."

Knock-knock!
    Who's there?
Mongoose.
    Mongoose who?
Mongoose is cooked!

HARE-LARIOUS

HETTY: Who controls congested rabbit highways?
BETTY: Hare Traffic Controller.

JEFF: What happened to the suicidal rabbit that
jumped off the ledge?
STEPH: He landed on a hare net.

MIA: How do you tell when a rabbit's going bald?
TIA: By its receding hare line.

JON: How did the rabbits survive the car crash?
DON: Dual Hare Bags.

How do rabbits keep cool in the summer?
Central hare conditioning.

How do Boy Scout whales start fires?
They rub two fish sticks together.

What happened to the gopher who grew his own herb garden?
He's having the thyme of his life.

What Australian mammal can transport up to 40 people?
A platy-bus.

What goes "quack-quack" and lives in the wilds of Alaska?
A Klon-duck.

Why did the silly squirrel bring home a box of ropes?
He was storing knots for the winter.

Father horse to son: "What happened to that girl you were going to marry?"

"She got colt feet."

Why did the elephant wear purple underwear?
His blue ones were at the laundromat.

GENE: What goes "Boom-squish, boom-squish, boom-squish"?
IRENE: A brontosaurus with wet sneakers.

What did the farmer get when he cut his cow in two?
Half and half.

FLOYD: What do you get when you cross a cat with a porcupine?
LLOYD: An animal that goes "meowch" whenever it licks itself.

What has feathers and observes underwater marine life?
Jacques Goose-teau.

How do antelopes keep in touch with the world?
They watch "The Evening Gnus."

Knock-knock!
Who's there?
Bison.
Bison who?
Bison, I'm going to miss you.

2. FAST-FOOD FUNNIES

What's a food lover's favorite magazine?
Eater's Digest.

CUSTOMER: I'm so hungry I could eat a horse.
WAITRESS: Oh, you heard about today's specials?

Little Sara watched as her mother stuck a meat thermometer inside the turkey.

"You're not going to get me to eat that!" she said, making a sour face.

"Why not?" asked her mother.

"Because if it's that sick," said Sara, "I don't want any."

What is it called when Chinese food takes a dive off a ten-story building?
Chop Suey-cide.

What is the difference between a person who eats other people and a container of beef?
One's a cannibal, the other's a can of bull.

What is the difference between a fast eater, a shoe-maker, and a person with a pebble in his shoe?
One's a gobbler, one's a cobbler, and one's a hobbler.

FAVORITE FIZZIES

What kind of soda do they drink?
Australian mammals drink Coca-Koala.
Ranchers drink Mountain Dude.
Optometrists drink Dr. Peeper.
Angels drink Heaven Up.
Surgeons drink Slice.
Beggars drink Cherry Coax.
Sailors drink Pep-sea.
Lambs drink Ewe-Hoo (Yoo-Hoo).
Zombies drink Canada Die.
Computer programmers drink Apple Cyber.

What are the favorite mints of English statesmen?
Parlia-mints.

MARY: What has chunks of meat, carrots, and pota-toes and hides out on cruise ships?
GARY: Stew-away.

What vegetable has a black belt in karate?
  Bruce Leek.

How do you fuel a vegetable-powered car?
  Fill it up with aspara-gas.

FLIP: How do you know when there's an elephant in your chocolate pudding?
FLOP: It's lumpier than usual.

CUSTOMER: Hey, there's a lot of fat on this menu!
WAITER (taking out a towel): Sorry. Here, let me wipe it off.

What swings through the trees and tastes good with milk?
  Chocolate chimp cookie.

CUSTOMER: Waiter, there are 49 flies in my soup.
WAITER: One more and we'll beat the world record.

What do you call Egg Foo Young after it's been sitting in your refrigerator for a month?
  Egg Foo Old.

The food at the convenience store in my neighborhood is so old the expiration dates are stamped in Roman numerals.

LANA: What cool-sounding food makes your tongue hot?
DANA: Chili.

MINA: Have you tried the new Hollywood citrus soda with half the calories of regular soda?
TINA: What's it called?
MINA: Lime-lite.

What is a sled dog's favorite food?
Mushed potatoes.

ZIGGY: What happened to the mad chef who tried to make pancakes in a volcano?
IGGY: He blew his stack.

STAN: Why did the silly driver suddenly get a craving for potato chips?
DAN: He saw a sign on the road that said "Dip Ahead."

CUSTOMER: Waiter, why is there a frog in my drink?
WAITER: Because things go better with croak.

In what kind of restaurant would you never find a vampire?
A stake house.

What do you get if you cross a honey cracker with a National Park?
The Graham Canyon.

MAD PLATTERS!

LLOYD: What do musicians order when they eat out?
FLOYD: The Combo Platter.

HETTY: What do safecrackers order when they eat out?
BETTY: The Combination Platter.

RUDY: Why did the lamb like the buffet restaurant?
JUDY: Because the menu said "All Ewe Can Eat."

GENE: Why did the waiter serve the physician a
    peanut butter and cucumber sandwich?
IRENE: Because that's just what the doctor ordered.

Wise man says, "Eat dinner in a minefield and you'll
get a bang out of dessert."

Customer to attendant at fast-food restaurant:
    "How much for a large Coke?"
    "A dollar fifty."
    "How much for a refill?"
    "Refills are free."
    "Great, just give me a refill."

BLAIR: What do you get when you mix eggs, cheese,
    and poison, and bake it in a pie crust?
CLAIR: I don't know, but it sounds like the quiche of
    death.

3. "YOU HAVE THE RIGHT TO REMAIN SILLY..."

Why were the cops called when the chicken failed to cross the road?

Fowl play was suspected.

When Mr. Bumble saw an ad in the paper that said, "Pedigreed police dog for sale, $40," he went to the pet store and plunked his money on the counter.

A few moments later the owner brought out the mangiest-looking dog Mr. Bumble had ever seen.

"You call this a pedigreed police dog?" huffed Mr. Bumble angrily.

"Don't be fooled by his looks," reassured the owner. "He's really in the Secret Service."

MOE: Did you hear there's a new movie about a convict who escapes from Alcatraz during a tornado?
JOE: What's it called?
MOE: Con with the Wind.

Where do you lock up bad gray matter?
In brain cells.

What type of cars do gangsters prefer?
Ones with semi-automatic transmission.

ZIGGY: Is it true that terrorists hid weapons in a baseball stadium?
IGGY: If it's true, then the bases really are loaded.

DILL: Who tells everyone he gives to the poor, but keeps it all to himself?
WILL: Robin Hoodwink.

Knock-knock!
   Who's there?
Alibi.
   Alibi who?
Alibi buy you some flowers if you open the door.

Knock-knock!
   Who's there?
Felon.
   Felon who?
Felon my head and got three stitches!

SUE: What is a burglar's favorite midnight snack?
LEW: Cheese and safecrackers.

What did the cat major in at the police academy?
Claw Enforcement.

What do court clerks eat for breakfast?
Oath-meal.

NIT: What's half man and half metal, sleeps on park benches by day, and fights crime by night?
WIT: Hobo-Cop.

LLOYD: How did you enjoy that video about the pastry murderer?
FLOYD: It was a real who-donut.

What kind of drawings do you find in prison art studios?
Finger prints.

What did the security guard say to the firefly?
"Halt! Who glows there?"

The boss of a big burglary operation was breaking in a new thief.

"Tonight, we're going to rob the lingerie company," said the boss to the rookie. "And remember—this time no slips."

What game do gangsters play?
Racket-ball.

What is a hangman's favorite magazine?
Noose Week.

Why did the cop arrest the lamb?
For making a ewe turn.

Knock-knock!
Who's there?
Justice.
Justice who?
Justice I thought. You broke my piggy bank!

LLOYD: What position do lawyers play on a football
team?
FLOYD: Defensive end.

What goes "Quack-quack!" and fights crime?
Duck Tracy.

LEM: What happens to cats when they get out of
prison?
CLEM: They go on purr-ole.

MINDY: Did you enjoy reading "The Pretzel
    Murders"?
CINDY: Yes, and I especially liked the twist ending.

What TV lawyer defends animals?
  Furr-y Mason.

Why was the Tupperware salesman ruled out as a
murder suspect?
  He had an airtight alibi.

WIFE to lawyer husband: How was court, dear?
HUSBAND: I had a very trying day.

What happened to the nearsighted cop who went to a
costume party?
  He couldn't tell the good guise from the bad guise.

SILLY PRISONER #1: I hear you're in prison because you're a sentimental guy.
SILLY PRISONER #2: That's right. I put my mother's picture on the twenty-dollar bills I was making.

VIDEOS FROM THE PRISON LIBRARY

Prison Break, starring Doug A. Tunnel
Life Sentence, starring Noah Parole

Some clever prisoners dug an escape route underneath the prison wall. The tunnel was so successful they put a toll booth in it.

Did you hear about the absentminded hit man? He took a body to the laundry and threw his clothes in the river.

Warden to death row prisoner:
    "Any last requests?"
    "Yes, I'd like a cigarette."
    "Are you crazy? That stuff'll kill you!"

MOTORCYCLE COP: Sir, were you in high gear when you had the accident?
SILLY DRIVER: No, I was in my tennis gear.

How do you tell the difference between a bad undercover cop and a good boxer?
    One blows his cover, the other covers his blows.

GERT: Which color isn't afraid to take a lie detector test?
BERT: True blue.

HERE COMES THE JUDGE!

JUDGE: The charge is stealing a blanket. How do you plead?
CROOK: Not quilty.

JUDGE: The charge is stealing a deck of cards.
CROOK: But, Your Honor...
JUDGE: Two months of solitaire.

JUDGE: I'm afraid I'm going to have to charge you.
SUSPECT: Fine, do you take Visa or MasterCard?

JUDGE: The charge is stealing wire posting.
MAN: But, Your Honor, it's my first of-fence.

JUDGE: Why did you steal the lamp?
CROOK: It wasn't very bright, was it?

The mad bomber's accomplice decided to call the police and inform them that there was a bomb in the building. In the nick of time, three men, five women, and a child were safely evacuated and the bomb defused.

The next day the newspaper headline read: "Snitch in Time Saves Nine."

TUTTI: My uncle broke out of prison.
FRUTTI: My uncle broke out in a rash.

How did the beautician break out of prison?
With a lock of hair.

DEX: What kind of duck picks locks?
LEX: A safequacker.

RUDY: Why did the judge place the eel on probation?
JUDY: It plead guilty to a lesser charge.

Cop to graffiti victim: "What was your reaction when the vandals spray-painted your house?"
    "I saw red."

LAWYER: Your Honor, I object! My client didn't mean to steal the yardstick.
JUDGE: Sorry—overruled!

HOMER: Why are bananas lawyers' favorite fruit?
GOMER: Because they like a-peels.

CLARA: How come they never search for crooks in churches?

SARA: Because crime doesn't pray.

HILARIOUS HOLDUPS

Why did the musician rob the savings and loan?
For the bank notes.

Why did the robber steal a crate of fat ducks?
He heard they had big bills.

PRISON WARDEN: How would you like to celebrate your birthday?

PRISONER: How about an open house?

After a long, frustrating day, the bank teller was eager to go home and get some rest. A minute before closing, a robber slowly approached the counter.

Reaching into his pocket, he fumbled for the gun and note.

"What are you trying to do?" said the teller, checking his watch, "hold me up?"

"Yes," snapped the robber, "that's exactly what I'm trying to do."

How did the computer hacker break out of prison using a PC?
He pressed the escape key.

A burglar broke into a house and stole a man's money and dentures. When he was arrested, the police gave him a polygraph test and found he was lying through somebody else's teeth.

POLICE CHIEF: Keep an eye on the beach. We've had reports of someone stealing surfboards.
OFFICER: Wow, chief, sounds like a crime wave.

What do you get if you cross a London policeman with a nanny?
A bobby sitter.

Did you hear about the judge who was so tough the only decoration in his office was hanging plants?

TUTTI: What would you get if you crossed an umpire with a burglar?
FRUTTI: Someone who breaks into your home and yells, "Safe!"

ZIP: My uncle's in jail for opening a convenience store.

ZAP: Since when is opening a convenience store a crime?

ZIP: He opened it with a crowbar.

LENNY: Last night I had my wallet stolen right out from under my nose.

BENNY: Next time keep your wallet in your pocket.

Prisoner to new cellmate:
"What are you in for?"
"Driving too slow."
"You mean too fast?"
"No, too slow. If I had been driving faster, they wouldn't have caught me."

Traffic cop to driver:
"Why were you speeding?"
"Because my brakes are bad and I wanted to get home before I had an accident."

Cop to bank teller:
"Are you sure it was an elephant that robbed the bank?"
"No, I can't be sure."
"Why not?"
"It had a stocking on its head."

What wish did the safecracker's mother have for her son?
"Locks of luck!"

4. WIGGLY GIGGLES

What's a worm's favorite chewing gum?
Wiggley's Spearmint Gum.

What did the worm say when it ate its way into the cucumber?
"I'm really in a pickle now!"

Why did the robin wear a necklace to breakfast?
Because the pearly bird gets the worm.

Momma Worm to neighbor: "I don't know what's wrong with my husband. He has no backbone."

BEN: My pet snake crawled into the garbage disposal.
KEN: Well, I guess it won't be long now.

TEACHER: Lou, how many feet would you have if you combined an eight-foot snake with a five-foot snake?

LOU: None. Snakes don't have feet.

What's the difference between a child's toy and a newborn snake?

One's a baby rattler, the other's a rattler's baby.

What rattler wrote the world's greatest plays?

William Snakespeare.

DANA: I found a baby snake in my garage.

LANA: Wow, what kind of shape was it in?

DANA: It was long and thin.

What kind of cheese do snakes like?

Shedder cheese.

SUE: What do you call a snake in a hard hat?
LEW: A boa constructor.

CLINT: Where would you go to find lost venomous
    snakes?
FLINT: The Missing Poisons Bureau.

What snake lures children with the sound of its flute?
    The Pied Viper.

A frog went to visit a fortune teller. "What do you see
in my future?" asked the frog.
    "Very soon," replied the fortune teller, "you will
meet a pretty young girl who will want to know
everything about you."
    "That's great!" said the frog, hopping up and down
excitedly. "But when will I meet her?"
    "Next week in science class," said the fortune teller.

What did one frog say to the other?
    "May I have a wart with you?"

What kind of mall sales attract fish?
    Back to school sales.

What did the mother fish say to the baby fish?
    "I haddock up to here with you!"

What kind of CDs do fish listen to?
    Sole music.

What do fireflies shout before takeoff?
    "All systems glow!"

Five insects rented rooms on the top floor of an apartment building while five rented rooms on the lower floor. What are these insects called?
Ten-ants.

How do you tell the difference between a person who has hope and an insect that leaves the hive?
One's a believer, the other's a bee leaver.

What would you get if you crossed a long-legged insect with a donkey?
A braying mantis.

What did one termite say to the other?
"Want to share a house with me?"

JILL: What is it called when one moth saves another moth from drowning?
DILL: Moth-to-moth resuscitation.

MACK: I caught an eel with my fishing rod.
JACK: Were you surprised?
MACK: Surprised? I got a big charge out of it.

Did you hear about the eel that got loose at the mall? It went on a shocking spree.

CHAD: What do you call a vehicle that seats two whales in the front and two whales in the back?
BRAD: I don't know, but it sounds like a four-whale drive.

TIP: What do you call an octopus with eight wallets?
TOP: The world's best pickpocket.

DANA: What's the difference between a noisy crustacean and a cranky violin player?
LANA: One's a fiddler crab, the other's a crabby fiddler.

What baseball-playing spider has the highest batting average?
Ty Cobb Web.

What kind of bee is always dropping the football?
A fumblebee.

RICH: How do you steal sweets from a bee?
MITCH: You walk up and say, "Your honey or your life!"

MANDY: I'm reading a story about a turtle that falls in love with a toupee.
SANDY: What it's called?
MANDY: The Tortoise and the Hair.

CLINT: What happened to the turtle that stepped on an electric wire?
FLINT: He got shell-shocked.

How did the fish plead before the judge?
Gill-ty.

RICH: How do you tell a fish to keep quiet?
MITCH: Say, "Shad-up already!"

What kind of whale is always gossiping?
A blubber mouth.

Why did the bat enter therapy?
To cure his hang-ups.

CHICK: Who do you call when there's a fly epidemic?
RICK: The Swat team.

5. GRUESOME GROANERS

ZIP: What do you call a sorceress with a broken broom?

ZAP: A witch-hiker.

SNIP: What do you get if you cross nursery rhymes with scary stories?

SNAP: Mother Goosebumps.

STU: Why do gnomes carry plenty of spare change?

LOU: For the troll booth.

What stories do baby werewolves listen to at bed-time?

Furry Tales.

NIT: What happened to the monster that ate the Christmas tree?
WIT: He had to get a tinsel-ectomy.

SUE: What evil crone turns off all the lamps on Halloween?
LEW: The light's witch.

GHOUL ZED: Who shall I invite to our Halloween party?
GHOUL TED: Anyone you can dig up.

Knock-knock!
    Who's there?
Freighter.
    Freighter who?
Freighter ghosts, are you?

Knock-knock!
    Who's there?
Howie.
    Howie who?
Howie know you're not a ghost?

FRANNY: Why did Godzilla hang out at the computer store on Halloween?
DANNY: So he could bob for Apples.

DAFFY: Why did King Kong climb to the top of the Empire State Building?
LAFFY: The elevator was broken.

SNIP: Who would you get to bury a dead clock?
SNAP: An under-ticker.

What do cannibals call kids on in-line skates?
Meals on Wheels.

VERN: Why did Wolfboy put his tooth under the pillow?
FERN: He was hoping for a visit from the Tooth Furry.

FIRST VAMPIRE: I heard the cops arrested you for trying to steal from the blood bank.
SECOND VAMPIRE: Yes, I got caught red-handed.

What does a cannibal call a meeting of the United Nations?
Variety pack.

VANCE: What do you get when you put the mind of a bunny into Frankenstein?
LANCE: A monster with a lot of hare-brained ideas.

Why did the two cannibals dash into the bookstore?
They saw a sign that said, "Meat the Authors."

Why did Captain Hook have trouble telling time?
His second hand kept falling off.

What monster plays the piano?
Frankensteinway.

What do dragons call brave knights?
Toast.

What do you get if you cross a leprechaun with a purple dinosaur?
Blarney.

What's big and green and overeats?
The Incredible Bulk.

What dinosaur built plastic toy buildings?
Lego-saurus.

What dinosaur has three horns and three wheels?
Tricycle-tops.

Did you hear about the alligator that proposed to Captain Hook?
She took his hand in marriage.

What do witches say when they cast the wrong spell?
"Hexcuse me!"

What is a zombie's favorite cereal?
Shred-dead Wheat.

CHRISSIE: Why did the big ape avoid sweets for a week?
MISSY: She was trying to watch her gorilla-ish figure.

What's a baby's favorite TV horror show?
Tales from the Crib.

Lem and Clem were close friends and bowling buddies for many years. One day they made a vow that whoever died first would send a message back to the other.

A week later Clem died and for many days Lem missed his bowling buddy. One night Clem's ghost appeared in Lem's bedroom.

"Tell me, Clem," said Lem excitedly, "is there bowling in heaven?"

"I have good news and bad news," replied Clem's ghost. "The good news is there's bowling every day."

"What's the bad news?" asked Lem.

"The bad news," said Clem, "is that starting tomorrow you're captain of the team."

Did you hear about the new build-it-yourself King Kong kit?
It comes with a monkey-back guarantee.

WILLIE: Who was the first dog dinosaur?
TILLIE: Terrier-dactyl.

What was Baby Godzilla's favorite crib toy?
A mobile home.

Knock-knock!
  Who's there?
Gatorade.
  Gatorade who?
Gatorade my grandmother.

A radioactive monster burst into a clothing store. "I can't keep my pants up," cried the monster. "Do you have any suspenders?"

"Sorry," replied the clerk. "But might I suggest a belt for your toxic waist?"

What do monsters play on a rainy day?
Musical Scares.

What don't zombies ever wear on boat trips?
Life jackets.

JACK: How did the zombie serve his country?
MACK: He joined the Peace Corpse.

What's Godzilla's favorite TV family?
The Brady...Munch!

RANDY: What's a dentist's favorite horror movie?
SANDY: "The Creature from the Plaque Lagoon."

MASON: Why is it so hard to celebrate Father's Day in Egypt?
JASON: Because there are more mummies than daddies.

NITA: What do you call the head of a vampire motorcycle gang?
RITA: Bleeder of the pack.

GENE: What do you get when you cross a dragon on Valentine's Day?
IRENE: Heartburn.

What position does King Kong play on the baseball field?

Any position he wants.

What monster sells hot dogs at baseball games?

Frankenfurter-stein.

What goes "Fee-fi-fo-fum, ho-ho-ho, crunch"?

A giant sitting on Santa Claus's lap.

What did the mad scientist get when he crossed an ostrich with a Big Mac?
A bird that buries its head in a sandwich.

What TV horror show features a host with a bad cough?
Tales from the Croup.

How did the Blob manage to get extra sleep in the morning?
When the alarm rang, he pressed the ooze button.

What's one place vampires don't mind getting locked up in?
Blood cells.

What do you get when you cross an African wild dog with a Halloween pumpkin?
A jackal-lantern.

What is a vampire's favorite dessert?
Leeches and cream.

At what mysterious vacation spot do crash dummies disappear without a trace?
The Bermuda Wreck-tangle.

DIT: Did you enjoy the movie "The Creature from the Gummy Lagoon"?
DOT: It stuck with me long after it was over.

What sea monster smells like cheese?
The Loch Ness Muenster.

CLARA: What do you give a mummy for Christmas?
SARA: Gift wrap.

FLIP: Why did the Wolfman need glasses?
FLOP: He was fur-sighted.

FUZZY: Why did the monster help the little old ghoul across the street?
WUZZY: Because that's what fiends are for.

What did the mummy say when the archaeologist discovered his tomb?
"For a while there, I thought I was a lost gauze."

FIRST ZOMBIE: Can I come to your autopsy party at the funeral parlor?
SECOND ZOMBIE: Sure, the morgue the merrier.

Where do they clone funny dinosaurs?
Joke-assic Park.

Who made the monster's wish come true?
The Scary Godmother.

What monster soaps windows on Halloween?
Prank-enstein.

VERN: What would you get if you crossed Godzilla with a Girl Scout?
FERN: I don't know, but I bet he sells a lot of cookies!

Who wears a mask and digs up dinosaur skeletons?
The Bone Ranger and Bronto.

HOMER: Why did the vampire flunk out of art class?
GOMER: Because he could only draw blood.

LEM: What do you get when you cross Godzilla with the Invisible Man?
CLEM: A great big nothing!

CLINT: What position did the Invisible Man play on the baseball team?
FLINT: No one knows.

Who's the most fearsome barber on Elm Street?
Freddy Crew-cut.

6. CRAZY QUESTIONS & CLEVER COMEBACKS

LENNY: Where does Batman keep his goldfish?
BENNY: In the bat tub.

MARY: What's the difference between a fly and an elephant?
GARY: You can't zip an elephant.

LEN: What's the difference between an expensive cat and one that does whatever you tell it to?
BEN: One's pedigree-able, the other's an agreeable pet.

CHUCKIE: What happened to the cat that swallowed a ball of wool?
BUCKIE: It had mittens.

DANA: What did the man say when the bird hauled his car away?
LANA: "Pigeon towed me."

JIM: How do you tell the difference between a friendly dog and a marine biologist?
SLIM: One's a tail wagger, the other's a whale tagger.

TIM: What did Noah say when the cows climbed onto the Ark?
JIM: "Now I herd everything!"

DILLY: How do you tell the difference between a wild Australian dog and people who like to gamble in church?
SILLY: One's a big dingo, the others dig bingo.

What do you call mad dogs rafting down the river?
White water rabids.

STAN: What kind of dog wakes up with its hair all messed?
DAN: Poodles. They get up curly in the morning.

STUDENT DRIVER: How did I do squeezing into that space?

DRIVING COACH: Not bad. But next time try parking on top of a sturdier car.

RICH: What's the difference between auto engine coolant and a snowbound female relative?

MITCH: One's an anti-freeze, the other's a freezing auntie.

GOMER: What do steering wheels and stool pigeons have in common?

HOMER: Sooner or later, they both turn on you.

DAD: Honey, I can't find my carpentry tools.

MOM: Oh, don't be such a saw loser.

What brand of mouthwash do grouchy people use?
Lister-mean.

NIT: How did the pair of scissors manage to win the
  race?
WIT: Shear energy.

TUTTI: How do you prevent water from getting into
  your house?
FRUTTI: Stop paying the water bill.

NITA: What did Godzilla's mother say when her baby
  ate the pig farm?
RITA: "Son, the sty's the limit."

SUE: Yesterday I saw an orange in the romance sec-
  tion of the bookstore.
LEW: What was an orange doing there?
SUE: Looking for a juicy novel.

KELLY: What is the difference between a sewing
  machine and a kiss on the lips?
TELLY: One sews seams nice, the other seems so nice.

How did the volcano sign its Mother's Day cards?
"Lava, your son."

SARA: Why do you call your boyfriend Domino?
CLARA: Because he's such a pushover.

NIT: My parents went away on a mystery weekend.
WIT: Where did they go?
NIT: I don't know—that's the mystery.

The boy was scared when he reached the top of the ledge. Two thousand feet below him lay rocky, treacherous waters. Suddenly several spectators began shouting, "Jump! Jump! Jump!"

Unable to bear it any longer, the boy plunged off the cliff, screaming all the way down. Fortunately, the boy is alive today and still likes to recount what happened that day on the cliffside. How did the boy survive?

He was a bungee jumper.

DAZE OF THE WEEK

What's a lifeguard's favorite day of the week?
Sand-day.

What is an astronaut's favorite day of the week?
Moon-day.

What are twins' favorite day of the week?
Two's day.

What day of the week do brides always look forward to?
Weds-day.

What day of the week makes your mouth dry?
Thirst-day.

What day of the week is a short order cook's favorite?
Fry-day.

What day of the week is a lazy person's favorite?
Sat-urday.

JEFF: Where can you drive without a license?
STEPH: On a golf course.

CLARA: Did you pass your driver's test?
SARA: I had a problem with the windshield.
CLARA: What happened?
SARA: The examiner's nose put a crack in it.

RICH: What is the difference between a geologist and a jerk?
MITCH: One has his head in the rocks, the other has rocks in his head.

LLOYD: Guess what I found when I traced my family tree?
FLOYD: A lot of dead wood?

MOM: How did you like the bookends I got you for your birthday?
TOM: I haven't had a chance to read them yet.

DILLY: Did you ever see a houseplant?
SILLY: No, but I saw bacon strip.
WILLY: That's nothing, I heard grass mown.
BILLY: I got you all beat. I saw a computer drive.

I'm so poor the secret code for my bank card is B-R-O-K-E.

What did Picasso's mother say when he threw a fit over his missing paint set?
   "Tempera, tempera!"

What kind of crow sticks to everything?
  Vel-crow.

What's a Labrador retriever's favorite writing toy?
  Fetch-a-Sketch.

What did the car say to the fast curve?
  "It was a pleasure swerving you."

What do you get if you cross a cat with an automobile?
  A car that cleans itself.

Where do old car tires end up?
  On skid row.

GERT: What do you call a dollar bill with no clothes on?
BERT: Buck naked.

DAFFY: I dropped a glass on the floor and didn't spill a single drop of water.
LAFFY: How did you do that?
DAFFY: It was a glass of root beer.

MUTT: Someday I want to be cloned.
JEFF: Why make another fool of yourself?

ANDY: What did the rip say to the pair of pants?
SANDY: "Well, I'll be darned!"

7. CHANNEL CHUCKLES

LEM: How do mice know what's playing at the movies?

CLEM: They watch "Squeak Previews."

DANA: The other day I sat through a terrible movie.

LANA: Why didn't you walk out?

DANA: I was going to, but the flight attendant wouldn't give me a parachute.

What is Arnold Schwarzenegger's favorite cereal? *Raisin Brawn.*

JILL: What rating did the movie critics give "The Secret Garden"?
PHIL: Two Green Thumbs Up.

What adventure movie features swashbuckling squirrels?
The Tree Musketeers.

What's the difference between a cartoon character that steals picnic baskets and a guru in the shower?
One's Yogi Bear, the other's a bare Yogi.

What's blue and works in a newsroom?
Smurfy Brown.

WHAT ARE THE CRITICS SAYING ABOUT...

"The Attack of the Killer Crows"?
The critics are raven!

"The Abominable Snowman"?
A real chiller.

"The Invisible Man"?
It's a must-see.

"The Snoring Monster"?
A real sleeper.

MINDY: Did you enjoy the movie about the porcupine?
CINDY: Up to a point.

GAME SHOWSTOPPERS

ZIP: How do "Wheel of Fortune" contestants give up?

ZAP: They throw in the vowel.

NED: What game show features skaters competing for prizes?

FRED: The Ice Is Right.

NITA: What is a clockmaker's favorite game?

RITA: Tick-Tock-Dough.

What's an elf's favorite TV sitcom?
Gnome Improvement.

What would you get if you crossed a TV buff with a baby kangaroo?
A pouch potato.

TED: Why was Rip Van Winkle upset when he woke up?

ED: His video rentals were overdue.

What's Godzilla's favorite snack?
Couch potato salad.

CHICKIE: What cartoon dog can be found on your lawn early in the morning?

DICKIE: Scooby Dew.

LOU: What do you get when you cross a paleontologist with a cartoon detective?

STU: Dig Tracy.

What TV news show do ghosts enjoy?
Entertainment Tomb-night.

What kind of family spends its time collecting CDs?
A disk-functional family.

ZIGGY: What has four heads, goes forwards and backwards, and eats ants?
IGGY: A VCRdvark.

ZIP: The world's dumbest robber broke into our house and stole the TV remote.
ZAP: So what's so bad about that?
ZIP: Every time he passes our house he changes channels.

MUSIC MANIA

What's a ghost's favorite kind of music?
   Rhythm and Boos.

What's the best way to find a screeching rock
star?
   With a Heavy Metal detector.

What kind of music goes "Fizz-fizz, bubble-bubble!"
   Pop music.

What kind of music do sad landscapers listen to?
   Blue grass.

What kind of music do chemists listen to?
   Acid Rock.

What music do bungee jumpers listen to?
   Big Band.

What music do baseball players listen to?
   Just the hits.

ANDY: Did you see the new James Bond movie where he falls into a huge vat of ice cream?
SANDY: No, what's it called?
ANDY: "Spy à la mode."

ZIP: Did you hear about the new Broadway musical with the singing and dancing sardines?
ZAP: I hear the show is really packing them in.

JOE: What would you do if a 500-pound gorilla sat in front of you at the movies?
FLO: Miss most of the movie.

MOM: How's the school play going?
TOM: Pretty well.
MOM: Is it a comedy or tragedy?
TOM: If lots of people come, it'll be a comedy. If no one comes, it'll be a tragedy.

What is the difference between a good set of speakers and a person who replaces house shingles?
One's a woofer, the other's a roofer.

After the rock band had finished the audition number, the record promoter scratched his head and said, "You're music's too loud, your lyrics are too crude, and the lead singer sounds like a cat screeching in a cactus patch."

"But what do you really think?" asked one of the band members.

"I'll think you'll sell a million," beamed the promoter, handing over the contract. "Sign here."

What did the compact disk player say to the CD?
"Wanna go for a spin?"

IGGY: Do you watch the classical music channel?
ZIGGY: If there's one thing I can't stand, it's too much
sax and violins.

MOE: Did you hear about the absentminded singing
waiter?
JOE: No, what did he do?
MOE: He tossed a ballad and sang a salad.

How do bakers square-dance?
They dough-si-dough.

What's Santa Claus's favorite cable program?
St. Nick at Nite.

8. NUTTY KNEE-SLAPPERS

TIFFANY: Why did you break up with that poet?
MELANIE: I just couldn't stanza him anymore.

BEETLE: Did you hear about the soldier who took a
  magic course and made a tank disappear?
BAILEY: How did he do that?
BEETLE: He used sleight of hand grenade.

Knock-knock!
  Who's there?
Spillane.
  Spillane who?
Spillane to me what's going on.

NUTTY NUCLEAR CROSSES

What would you get if you crossed a nuclear plant with...

A duck?
Melt-down.

A wooden puppet?
Pin-nuke-io.

A movie star?
Nuclear re-actor.

WHO SAID IT?

"I'm stuck on you!"
A wad of gum talking to a tennis shoe.

"I'm attracted to you!"
Metal talking to a magnet.

"You rub me the wrong way!"
A chalkboard talking to an eraser.

"I feel so drained!"
A bathtub talking to water.

"Just a little off the top, please."
Grass talking to a lawn mower.

Knock-knock!
   Who's there?
Colt.
   Colt who?
Colt outside, you better wear a jacket.

What brand of diapers do mother cats prefer?
   Pam-purrs.

HOMER: What has eight flippers, two beach balls, and
   rides a bicycle built for two?
GOMER: Seals on wheels.

MINDY: Why was the cockatoo first in line at the
   beauty parlor?
CINDY: Because the early bird gets the perm.

SILLY SLEEPERS

LLOYD: Where do detectives sleep?
FLOYD: Under cover.

RUDY: What type of bed do fighters prefer?
JUDY: Box springs.

MARY: What do eels sleep under?
GARY: Electric blankets.

Knock-knock!
  Who's there?
Dots.
  Dots who?
Dots for me to know, and you to find out.

CRAZY CAMPS

What did you learn at...

Frog Camp?
  Warts and Crafts.

Zombie Camp?
  Swimming, but no lifesaving.

Demolition Camp?
  Home Wreckonomics.

Jelly Camp?
  Jam-nastics.

How did the three poor woodcarvers manage to buy a Mother's Day gift?

They all chipped in.

PETAL PUNS

What kind of flowers do you give a monster?

Mari-ghouls and morning gories.

What kind of flowers do you give an absentmind-ed squirrel?

Forget-me-nuts.

What kind of flowers do you give to someone who sleeps all the time?

Day-zzzzz's.

MACK: How do you find flowers on a beach?
JACK: With a petal detector.

Knock-knock!
  Who's there?
Hawaii.
  Hawaii who?
I'm fine, Hawaii you?

NIFTY SWIFTIES

"I'll never pet an alligator again," said Captain Hook offhandedly.

"The teacher's giving us an exam today," said Larry testily.

Did you hear the joke about the airplane?
　　Never mind, it's over your head.

Nervous airline passenger to flight attendant:
　　"Miss, do these planes crash very often?"
　　"Oh, no, sir! They only crash once."

THE WORLD'S SILLIEST EPITAPH

Ebenezer Bell fell down a well
And broke his collarbone.
Take his advice and always think twice,
　　And leave well enough alone.

Knock-knock!
　　Who's there?
Aaron.
　　Aaron who?
Aaron out my smelly gym shoes.

Knock-knock!
　　Who's there?
Candice.
　　Candice who?
Candice be the last knock-knock joke?

Knock-knock!
　　Who's there?
Moira.
　　Moira who?
Moira jokes to come!

9. FROM GAGS TO STITCHES

DILLIE: Why did the sick skunk stay in bed for a week?
DALLIE: Doctor's odors.

Why did the ghost go the hospital?
To have his ghoul-stones removed.

What do germs wear when they get up in the morning?
Mic-robes.

What did the vet put on the pig's pimple?
Oinkment.

RANDY: Why don't aardvarks get sick?
SANDY: They're full of anty-bodies.

Knock-knock!
   Who's there?
Dispatch.
   Dispatch who?
Dispatch on my eye makes it hard to see.

FOOD FOR THOUGHT

PATIENT (Monday morning): Doctor, I think I'm a carrot. What should I do?

DOCTOR: Take these pills and see me on Wednesday.

PATIENT (Wednesday morning): Doctor, I think I'm a lima bean.

DOCTOR: Take these pills and see me on Friday.

PATIENT (Friday morning): Doctor, today I think I'm a cabbage.

DOCTOR: You'd better quit while you're a head.

ZIGGY: What disease would you get if you crossed a hen with a Vulcan?
IGGY: Chicken Spocks.

SILLY SICKNESS!

What disease do they get?

> *Hockey players get the chicken pucks.*
> *Antelopes get gnu-monia.*
> *Frogs get hop-atitis.*
> *Vampires have coffin fits.*
> *Rats get sewer throats.*
> *Monsters get scare-let fever.*

COUNSELOR: Your mother tells me you keep trying to run away from home. What stops you?

SHANA: Well, every time I get to the front door, the phone rings.

Charlie's doctor was a real quack. One day Charlie went for a checkup and his doctor said, "Please strip to the waist."

When Charlie had removed his shirt, the doctor said, "When I hit you on the back, cough."

The doctor hit him on the back and Charlie coughed. For the next ten minutes he kept whacking Charlie and Charlie kept coughing.

Finally, the phony doctor shook his head and said, "How long have you had this cough, anyway?"

KRAMER: Doctor, how do I keep from losing my hair?

DOCTOR: Write your name on your toupee.

"Doctor, I keep seeing double."
   "Here, have a seat."
   "Which one?"

Kleptomaniac to doctor: "I have this terrible urge to
steal, especially everything that's marked down."
   "Like what?"
   "Last week, for example, I took home an elevator."

PATIENT: Thanks to you, doc, I'll never gamble again.
DOCTOR: Wanna bet?

PATIENT: Doctor, I'm going to kill myself!
QUACK: Wait!
PATIENT: Why?
QUACK: Did your pay your bill yet?

LENNY: Your doctor has terrible handwriting.
BENNY: Well, his prescriptions are hard to read, but
   his bill is nice and clear.

ANDY: My mom works at the Old MacDonald Farm
   Hospital.
SANDY: What does she do?
ANDY: She's in the emergency room.
SANDY: Oh, you mean the E-R-E-R-O?

WILLY: What's worse than mononucleosis?
DILLY: Stereo-nucleosis.

What did Julius Caesar's doctor say when Caesar
came down with the sniffles?
   "Hail, Sneezer!"

DOCTOR DILLIES

"Doctor, doctor, every night my foot falls asleep."
  "What's wrong with that?"
  "It snores."

"Doctor, doctor, I think I'm a trampoline!"
  "Don't worry, you'll bounce back in no time."

"Doctor, I think I have the Miniature Golf Disease."
  "Just let it run its course."

PATIENT: Last night I dreamed I was trapped
  inside a laundromat.
DOCTOR: What did you do?
PATIENT: What could I do? I tossed and turned.

PATIENT: Doctor, I keep having this nightmare
  that I'm a postage stamp.
DOCTOR: If we work together, we can lick this problem.

WOMAN: Doctor, doctor, I think I'm a gas pump.
DOCTOR: Stop acting fuelish.

WOMAN: My mother-in-law thinks she's a para-
  chute.
DOCTOR: What's wrong with that?
WOMAN: She keeps dropping in unannounced.

What medical advice did the doctor give
  Samson?
  "Take two pillars and call me in the morning."

DAN: My doctor says I have the Ferris Wheel Flu.
STAN: I heard there was something going around.

What did the puzzle piece say to the psychiatrist?
  "I don't fit in anymore."

What kind of exams does Dr. Pepper perform?
  Fizzi-cals (physicals).

WIFE: My husband constantly talks to himself.
DOCTOR: It's normal for people to talk to themselves.
WIFE: On the telephone?

DOCTOR: Did those pills I gave you improve your
  memory?
PATIENT: Yes, but who are you?

Wracked with fever, Benny rang Dr. Godfrey's door-bell at three in the morning. Dragging himself out of bed, the doctor opened the door and said, "Well?"

"No," replied Benny, "sick."

How do ducks relieve pain?
Quackupuncture.

TOM: Knock-knock!
MOM: Who's there?
TOM: Kleenex.
MOM: Kleenex who?
TOM: Kleenex are nicer than dirty necks.

Father Oyster was in the hospital room waiting to hear news of his expectant wife. When the nurse finally arrived, the Oyster asked anxiously, "What is it? Please tell me, what is it?"

"Congratulations!" beamed the nurse happily. "It's a pearl!"

TEACHER: How many bones are in your body?
HENRY: About 207.
TEACHER: No, only 206.
HENRY: Then how do you account for the chicken bone I swallowed at lunch?

TEACHER: Use the words "head lice" in a sentence.
KERRI: When you drive at night, it's important to turn on your head lice.

Why did the famous baseball player go to the dentist?
To have a Ruth canal.

What famous baseball player always had the sniffles?
Hankie Aaron.

10. ZANY ZOO ZINGERS

What happened to the zebra that got court-martialed?
She lost her stripes.

SLIM: It's feeding time at the zoo!
JIM: Better hurry or you'll be late for dinner.

Our zoo is so mixed up they crossed a cuddly bear with a hobo and got a panda-handler.

LEM: What do you get when you cross an elephant with a parrot?
CLEM: An animal that tells you everything it remembers.

What is black and white, black and white, and green?
Two zebras fighting over a pickle.

Knock-knock!
  Who's there?
Dewey.
  Dewey who?
Dewey have to give the hippo a bath?

CHUCKIE: Knock-knock!
DUCKIE: Who's there?
CHUCKIE: My panther.
DUCKIE: My panther who?
CHUCKIE: My panther falling down!

What kind of pictures do Arctic bears keep in their scrapbooks?
  Polar-oids.

"We'll never catch an elephant," sighed the first game hunter after a long day in the jungle. "Let's go home."
  "I agree," replied the second. "Besides, I'm exhausted from carrying these decoys."

One day a nearsighted wrestler and his friend were walking near a farm when a large bull reared up. Fearing for his friend's life, the wrestler grabbed the bull by the horns and wrestled it to the ground. Snorting angrily, the bull leaped up and ran off.

"Thanks for saving my life," sighed the friend.

"Don't worry," said the nearsighted wrestler. "If that guy ever comes back, I'll yank him off the bicycle and really show him who's boss."

KYLE: What has stripes, screams, and gets sick to its stomach?

LYLE: A zebra on a roller coaster.

NIT: I heard that pigs do their own laundry.

WIT: That's hogwash!

What's big and white and lives in the Sahara Desert?
A polar bear with a bad sense of direction.

What's black and white and pink all over?
A sunburned zebra.

MACK: What do you call a turkey the day after Thanksgiving?
JACK: Leftovers.

Where do ravens go to shoot pool?
Crow-bars.

What would you get if you crossed a sheep and an African monkey?
A baaaaa-boon.

SILLY HUNTER #1: Why are you sticking your head in that rabbit's mouth?
SILLY HUNTER #2: Just getting a breath of fresh hare.

How did the alley cat get to be leader of the pack?
He clawed his way to the top.

Why did the mole go to the bank?
To burrow money.

What's big and gray and jittery?
An elephant that drinks too much coffee.

ANDY: What position did the skunk play on the baseball team?
SANDY: Scenter field.

DANA: What's big and gray and doesn't have any
    friends?
LANA: An elephant with bad breath.

What's a polar bear's favorite vacation spot?
    Brrrrrrr-muda.

What do you call a polar bear in sunglasses?
    Radi-cool.

What would you get if you crossed a mechanic with a
kangaroo?
    Jumper cables.

What's gray, has one ear, and paints?
    Vincent Van Elephant.

11. WACKY WORK

GENE: What do overworked computer programmers do at the end of a long day?
IRENE: They go home and crash.

MARY: My mother sews, my father weaves, and my sister crochets.
GARY: Sounds like you have a close-knit family.

What's the difference between a hat maker and a boat turned upside down?

One sizes caps, the other capsizes.

SIGN OF THE TIMES
Window repairman motto

MOE: How's your uncle the hobo?
JOE: He got a job as a dishwasher.
MOE: Wow, he's gone from panhandling to handling pans.

SIGN AT A FALSE-TEETH CLINIC

What do plumbers eat for breakfast?
Wrench Toast.

82

What did the chef hate most about his job?
It was all wok and no play.

DIT: Whose job is it to drive all the customers away?
DOT: A limo driver.

JILL: My cat got a job with Xerox.
WILL: I guess that makes him a copy cat.

SIGN AT A SHOE REPAIR SHOP

SANDY: What's the difference between a prisoner and
a tennis instructor?
ANDY: One serves time, the other times serves.

VERN: My uncle's wife builds houses for a living.
FERN: I guess that makes her a carpenter aunt.

What did the minister shout when lightning struck the church?

"Holy smoke!"

What is the difference between a grocery clerk and a person who sells business shares?

One stocks the market, the other markets the stock.

LEM: My town is so small our fire department has a hose, a cart, and four dogs.

CLEM: What are the dogs for?

LEM: They know where to find the hydrant.

What does the president of the United States turn up when he wants his music louder?
  The Speaker of the House.

Sign at Bulletproof Glass Company:
  "We stand behind our work."

What kind of stories do bakers tell their children?
  Breadtime stories.

What is the difference between a nursemaid and a mountain climber?
  One rocks the cradle, the other cradles the rocks.

Where do Eskimo barbers live?
  In wig-loos.

Where do giant Eskimos live?
  In big-loos.

What do the seven dwarfs do when it's time for Chinese food?
  Whistle while they wok.

What happened to the lazy standup comic?
  He was fired for sitting down on the job.

Why do rubber bands make good soldiers?
  They snap to attention.

What would you get if you crossed a mountain lion with an ice cream truck?
  The Good Puma Man.

Who chops trees in his sleep?
A slumberjack.

HOW'S BUSINESS?

"Looking up!" said the elevator operator.
"Getting better all the time," said the doctor.
"Could be wurst," said the sausage factory owner.
"Picking up," said the trash collector.
"A bit sticky," said the glue manufacturer.

ZIP: Why did the King stop lending Humpty Dumpty money?
ZAP: Because no matter how much the King lent him, Humpty Dumpty was always broke.

RUDY: What did the wooden boy say to the barber?
JUDY: Just a whittle off the top.

86

Who is in charge of the Never Never Land Fire Company?

Captain Hook and Ladder.

FIRING LINES

What happened when they got fired?

The geologist hit rock bottom.
The garbage collector got down in the dumps.
The astronaut started moonlighting.
The baseball player struck out on his own.
The exterminator got ant-sy.
The computer programmer didn't have a byte in days.

VERN: How was your day at the lingerie shop?
FERN: I got the pink slip.

What is a computer programmer's favorite cookie?

Chocolate micro-chip.

What's a pizza maker's favorite motto?

"Cheesy come, cheesy go."

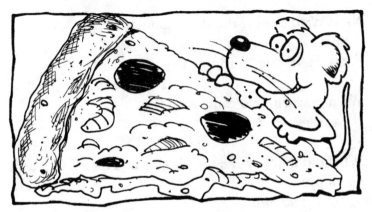

12. LAUGHED OVERS

FARMER DILL: Does your cow have bells around its neck?

FARMER WILL: Why should it have bells when it's already got two horns?

NED: Want to hear the story about the cattle round-up?

FRED: Herd one, herd them all.

What magazine do cattle read?
Cows-moo-politan.

What did the farmer's son shout when he fell into a vat of prunes?
"This is the pits!"

HILLYBILLY VERN: Honey, Jethro and I are going into the woods to shoot some dice.

HILLYBILLY FERN: Dice? But I don't know the first thing about cooking dice.

A man drove his car into the middle of a tornado and soon found himself spinning out of control. Before he knew it his car was dangling halfway over the edge of a cliff. Quickly, he dialed the police on his car phone and shouted, "Help! I'm caught in the storm."

"Don't worry," the dispatcher reassured him. "It'll blow over."

"That's exactly what I'm afraid of," wailed the man.

JERRI: How do Oriental rugs telephone each other?

TERRI: Persian-to-Persian.

SIGN AT A CLOCK REPAIR SHOP

WINNY: My pet wolf has a bad habit of hanging out with other wolves.

VINNY: What's wrong with that?

WINNY: He's up to two packs a day.

ZIP: Why did Godzilla own two compact cars?
ZAP: Because it's hard to roller-skate with just one.

A man who was hard of hearing was relaxing on a park bench when a boy came along walking his dog. Immediately, the dog began barking viciously at the man on the bench.

"Say, your dog didn't sleep so well last night," said the man.

"Why do you say that?" asked the boy.

"Can't you tell?" replied the man. "Every time he looks at me he yawns."

Knock-knock!
  Who's there?
Kenya.
  Kenya who?
Kenya loan me five dollars, I'm broke!

MINDY: How is a lazy dog like a steep mountain?
CINDY: One's a slow pup, the other's a slope up.

Anxious to get married, a young couple arrived at the minister's house at three o'clock in the morning. Waking the minister from a sound sleep, they persuaded him to perform the ceremony right away.

The next day the headline in the newspaper read: "Minister ties knot in his pajamas."

Why did the two volcanoes refuse to talk to each other?

They had a lava's quarrel.

LOONY STAMPS

Did you hear about the new postage stamps...?

The Little Rascal stamp?—It deserves a good licking.
The Athlete stamp?—It's so sweaty you don't have to lick it.
The Hermit stamp?—It sticks to itself.
The Welder's stamp?—If you can't lick it, join it.
The Santa Claus stamp?—Yule love it.
The Cat stamp?—It licks itself.
The Bugs Bunny stamp?—It's good for Hare Mail.
The Stork stamp?—It delivers itself.
The King Arthur stamp?—It's for over-knight delivery.
The Kindergarten stamp?—It's good for first class.
The Fog stamp?—It comes with postage dew.

A BRIEF RIDDLE

What is the difference between a person who gets two fives for a twenty, and a person who puts on clean underwear?

One gets short-changed, the other changes shorts.

Just in the nick of time the fire department arrived at a house engulfed in flames.

Rushing inside, one of the firemen pulled an absentminded professor from his bed and led him safely outside.

"That oughta teach you to smoke in bed!" said the fireman to the professor.

"Who was smoking?" coughed the professor. "That bed was on fire when I got into it."

A man with a bad case of laryngitis went to a hardware store to buy a hammer. Since he could barely speak, the man made a hammering motion with his hands. The hardware clerk quickly understood and sold the man a hammer.

Later, a shy boy arrived to buy a screwdriver for his father. Too timid to talk, the boy used his hands to make a twisting motion, and the clerk sold him a screwdriver.

Finally, a blind man came into the store to buy a saw. What did he do to show the hardware clerk what he needed?

The blind man simply asked for the saw.

Where do cows stay on vacation?
In moo-tels.

Knock-knock!
Who's there?
Albee.
Albee who?
Albee home for Christmas.

HOUSEKEEPER'S TOMBSTONE

Here lies the body of a girl named Gina,
Who bought a Hoover vacuum cleaner.
She got in the way
Of its suction one day.
Since then no one has seen her.

GOODBYE GIGGLES

LENNY: How do gardeners say goodbye?
BENNY: "Seed you later."

MISSY: How do tailors say goodbye?
CHRISSY: "Sew long."

SUE: How do pigs say goodbye?
LEW: With hogs and kisses.

Knock-knock!
  Who's there?
Shirley.
  Shirley who?
Shirley you could open the door for me.

Knock-knock!
  Who's there?
Sanctuary.
  Sanctuary who?
Sanctuary much for answering the door.

Knock-knock!
  Who's there?
Gladys.
  Gladys who?
Gladys is the last knock-knock joke!

About the Authors

Knock-knock!
  Who's there?
Author.
  Author who?
Author any more jokes by Matt and Phil?

Matt and Philip are the authors of *The Great Book of Zany Jokes* and the *Biggest Joke Book in the World,* both also published by Sterling. They have performed at schools, libraries, and hospitals for children. Recently, they were heard on the Peabody Award–winning radio program "Kids' Corner." Matt lives near Valley Forge, Pennsylvania, with his wife, Maggie, and daughters, Rebecca and Emily. Philip makes his home in Austin, Texas, with Maria and their cat, Sam.

About the Illustrator

Jeff Sinclair has been drawing cartoons ever since he could hold a pen. He won several local and national awards for cartooning and humorous illustration. When he is not at his drawing board, he can be found renovating his house and working on a water garden in the backyard. Jeff has gone into cyberspace on the Internet. He lives in Vancouver, British Columbia, Canada, with his wife, Karen, son, Brennan, daughter, Conner, and golden Lab, Molly.

Index